The Great Hike

The Great Hike
San Francisco to San Diego
September 26 - December 12, 1914
Copyright © 2022 by Anthony L. Rantz

All rights reserved. No part of this book may be reproduced or transmitted in any form or by any means without written permission from the publisher and author.

Additional copies may be ordered from the publisher for educational, business, promotional or premium use. For information, contact ALIVE Book Publishing at: alivebookpublishing.com, or call (925) 837-7303.

Cover Art by Cian Modena-Hayden
Book Design by Alex Johnson

ISBN 13
978-1-63132-160-3

First Edition

Published in the United States of America by ALIVE Book Publishing
an imprint of Advanced Publishing LLC
3200 A Danville Blvd., Suite 204, Alamo, California 94507
alivebookpublishing.com

PRINTED IN THE UNITED STATES OF AMERICA

10 9 8 7 6 5 4 3 2 1

The Great Hike

San Francisco to San Diego
September 26 - December 12 1914

Compiled by

Anthony L. Rantz

Alive Book Publishing

Publishing of this journal has been facilitated by
Anthony L Rantz.
Anthony would like to dedicate this book to
Richard and Ermadeanne Rantz,
who compiled all of Mary Rantz Schwab's
original journal entries together.

The Great Hike
San Francisco to San Diego
26 September – 12 December
1914

Notes typed from small notebook (no alterations or changes) carried by Mary Rantz Schwab on a "Great Hike".

She and her husband of two years, Rudolph Schwab, were hoping to do some union work and to discover what working conditions were like. They were active members of the Socialist-Labor Party in San Francisco.

She was 30 years old and he was 29

Compiled by Erma Deanne Rantz

FOOD EXPENSES

Food For Start 9/26

Macaroni	.10
Spuds	.10
Onions	.05
Soups	.70
Salami	.50
Coffee	.50
Tea	.20
Honey	.20
Mush	.20
Hotcakes	.15
Sugar	.15
Milk	.10
Tomato Sauce	.10
Bacon	.10
Candles	.10
	3.05

September 1914   19th

Rudolph and I make our first purchases. A grid, 1 army cup, straps, leggings, 2 tin pots, two tin plates, two knives, shoes, camp hatchet, hat for me. Kern lends us a knapsack, shelter tent - blanket - blanket - army frying pan - cup and he gives us much advice which he thinks is good.

September 20

Went to Phipps for dinner. Went to see Lou (half-brother) afterwards, was not home - working. Saw Marie and the baby.

September 21

Bought two pairs pants, underdrawers for myself. Will wear light vests however. R. and I practicing with Tinie's (R's sister) camera getting familiar with it, for we hope to mark our tramp with many interesting pictures. Wrote a letter home this evening.

September 23 8 p.m.

Am sitting on the edge of my bed with my feet in a tub of hot water in a room as hot as a bake oven, when I ought to be presiding at Trautman's first San Francisco meeting. Fortunately I had quit my work yesterday so I was perfectly free to entertain old Mr. LaGrippe who came during the night and which explains the hot foot bath tonight. I must master this visitation before tomorrow for tomorrow we make our start.

In spite of my indisposition I mended Rudolph's coat, sewed the ground flap on the tent and did various other necessary things preparing for our start. Weather foggy and cold today.

September 26

Trautman's meeting. We talked of staying over Saturday night but changed our minds and Saturday morning found us packed and ready to go. Took car to San Mateo (25 cents each). There while in dressing room, hair down, heard the distant whistle of approaching train. Pinned up hair, seized bag, sweater, blankets, rushed into men's waiting room. There sat Rudolph calmly repairing his gaiters. Caught train! Conductor overlooked our fares (saved fifty cents) Bought candles and soap. Asked road of ex-central flagman - fearful of moving objects. Struck LaHonda road. Passed through Woodside - lift to Searsville. Took Alpine Road and come to Francisquito Creek. Found ready made camp. Bathed feet - supper macaroni, pea soup, salami, coffee. Moonlight - went to bed then came the Twenty who broke up camp at 9:30 p.m. Stumbled on to Stubble field spread blankets. Went to sleep. Heard coyotes. Wakened at midnight. the twenty were departing.

FOOD EXPENSES

Milk —
2 dz apples —

September 27 Sunday

Breakfast - mush, cakes, and coffee. On road at 9 (late) Came to a fork and truck, asked direction (lumber truck). Left about 15 miles over divide to Pescadero creek headwaters. Took old Indian trail over ridge - virgin redwood. Lunch (canteen, salami, garlic bread). Blisters on heels. After four hours toiling over the ridge see a great boulder to the right Whangdooles Retreat Underneath "enter". Inside two dilapidated trundle beds, broken stove, broken homemade chair. Outside a stove, a rough leanto, table underneath and on table pots turned upside down. Down below a fine water hole. Only 3:30 so we decide to push on.

Trail steep up gulch, almost turned back, in ten minute climb find a road. Half hour up the road find a shake camp. House deserted, signs of habitiation - tomatoes, milk, dog barks. Italian directs us down the road two miles to Government Camp. Road runs on knife edge ridge - took picture of view. To our left, thousands feet the Big Basin. Ankle deep dust on road - come to Government Camp four miles down steep trail. Limestone 2 miles - down gulch - getting dark - come suddenly to favorable camping place - fine water. Redwood glade - supper by candle light slept on fern bed between two giant redwoods - moon rays through the trees, coyotes and the call of wild things.

September 28 (Monday)

Bread .05

Heels painfully sore, dress them in handkerchief sprinkled with powder. R. makes fire and breakfast in dim canyon light. Later sun sends golden shafts through the redwoods. Wash towel and handkerchiefs. Mend skirt and rent in R.s trousers. Solitude. (China Grade   Maddock Creek) Inn at Big Basin. Take trail to Boulder Creek. Indeterminate - Bathe in creek (Picture) Rest for an hour - resume trail. Deserted mill - ruined road - broken bridge, (picture) Find orchard-Old Irish farmer, apples. Rancher's house - chair - dressers. Divide down the road at dusk emerge on Santa Cruz county road --heels very sore -plod on-Trough and signs "Keep out - No camping". We camp. By candle and moon supper includes applesauce, bed of leaves, screened from road by trees. Night warm, early morning very cold - breakfast - make repairs to heels sterile dressing.

Tuesday the 29th

Glorious sunshine. Start at ten for Boulder, two miles west. Boulder Creek changed for better, in two years...Drug store - films, zinc ointment. Bread, place where two years back we got that excrable coffee. We limped out of Boulder to the little Tern Brook - back to the road - lift - Harris (Grant Ave) to Felton. Same old Felton. At corner saw Mrs. Slikerman and Silberly. Little house on hill again. Sleep on cot under open sky. Bath and treat our sore feet.

Wednesday 30th

Misty but beautiful morning. Breakfast, wash stockings and underwear. Familiar scolding of blue jays'. Supper at Solunds spend evening there. Rudolph and Dean recount stories of the Road.

Thursday October 1

Yellow jackets wake us at 6 a.m. After breakfast Mrs. S., R. and I go to Gold Gulch - placer mining there. Visit Guenters Dean Mrs S. Slept at Solunds indoors.

Old Indian Trail over the ridge into Big Basin

Mary on Indian Trail

Rudolph on Indian Trail

Watsonville Picking Apples

Old bridge after leaving Big Basin

Cowboy and Mary   Gonzales

Friday October 2

Bread .05
Can Tomatoes .10

Start for Santa Cruz (9 a.m.) Camp above Twin Lakes near Hotel Del Mar. Tent under eucalyptus; rain clouds. R.tranches tent. Sleep warm and comfortable. Slight drizzle. Moonlight towards morning. Marvelous sunrise. Go in swimming, take pictures - beach very treacherous. Went to Santz Cruz, bought fry pan, coffee pot, stockings and salami, milk, bread, called on Mrs. Livingood. Supper - back to camp by moonlight.

October 3

Salami .31
Bread .10
Borden's milk .20

Hatchet missing - break camp - on road again by 10 a.m. Wonderful blue sky, deep blue sea with surf dashing on rocks. Come to Capitola, a pleasant little resort. Get railroad map - on road to Aptos. Stop for lunch on beach under trees near track at New Brighton - only part of which we see, being the sign on it (Borden's milk proves unhandy) Aptos, old fashioned California town - three hotels, Bay View, Ocean House, Live Oak House. On the road from Aptos to Watsonville. Many apples but that is all. No water, no camping places. Hot white road, burning blue sky, parched yellow hills - tried to get come corn, parched and wormy. Rest under water tank (empty) eat apples. About four o'clock stop - packing plant and find a small ax. Strike settlement. Water trough - ask grocer where can camp. "out there under the trees", he replied indicating a few dusty apple trees along the road back of the store..our surprise and relief great. Cook supper; full yellow moon over ridge. Rudolph steals into neighboring field, gets bean straw. Sleep good.

October 4

apples —
3 ears corn —
1 qt milk —

Break camp at dawn, no breakfast. Lift part of way to Watsonville on road lined with apple trees, forests of apple trees. Cold clear morning - farmer tells of history of "Freedom" nicknamed Whiskey Hill, old Spanish settlement. Watsonville a farmers trading town.

Go through town, passed station at Watsonville Junction- Pajara river - mud flat. Come out on clean county road again. Then monotonous rolling plateau land on way to Moss Landing.

Lift to Salinas River, change plans, omitting Monterey. On our way towards San Luis Obispo. Pass Spreckel's Sugar Refinery. Fine schoolhouse - miles of sugar beets. Land owned by Spreckels, tenant farmers..Large wagons drawn by six-horse teams bearing beets to factory. Net unloading device. Pass Chualar on other side of Salinas River - river small spreading between sand flats. Noon - camp beneath dust laden live oak near dusty road. Dinner under difficulties high wind blows fire - cup lost - clean up and take wash in stream. River crawls through sand, waste, winding, losing itself. Wade mile up-stream - quicksands. Resume road, ankle deep dust strong trade winds - gently rolling road Big oak flats. Dairy ranch, alfalfa bloated cow-crude treatment. Get qt of milk. Go on towards Gonzales Camp in oaks behind dairy ranch. curious horses and cows. plenty hay M. gets cramps that night

October 6

Margin notes:
- 1 qt milk —
- 2½ cans alpine milk —
- Hamburger .10
- Cornmeal .15
- sugar .10
- Cards .05
- stamps .10
- 7-8 large apples —
- Plum Pie —
- Rabbit —
- 4.31

Given good creamy milk - road dusty - morning cool, misty. Lift at bridge on milk wagon. Gonzales boasts two streets, fair stores. Alpine Cream Plant. Wagons filled with milk cans from all directions - son of owner, J.P. Meyenburg(JBM) Swiss German inventor of process, started Carnation, cheated out of royalties, etc. - make complete tour of plant - drink milk - machine process throughout - 22½cents wages, indeterminate hours - sanitary to all appearances -labor saving devices throughout. Resume road - tired and hungry - stop gateway of ranch under windblown cypress - cook milk and cream of wheat + hamburger. four dirty children watch proceeding. Sugar beets on road going south. Resume road toward Soledad - ½ mile lift to Camphora-cross toward river in direction of Soledad Mission. Pie (Plum) from Kancho, Japanese cook on cook shack ofTraction Plow Gang. See steam plow. rabbit - make difficult progress across stream. camp in dusty willow grove near water trough. Supper stewed rabbit, macaroni and pie and coffee. Prepare for night(rain threatens) trench tent - no rain.

October 7

Margin notes:
- Bread .10
- 1 qt milk —
- 2 apples —
- 15 fine spuds —

Break camp 6:30 - dusty road, plowed fields, many barbed wire fences - came to Soledad Mission, a ruin amid thrifty peasants, haystacks in mission courtyard - walls and portals of adobe standing. Too foggy for pictures - Cross river for breakfast and wash up. Potato field, get fine spuds. After lunch and bathing recross river and fields at Mission. Take four pictures. On road again at 3 p.m.   Adobe road house - white - veranda - dating 1800, wood portion 1849. Bought bread 10¢ from vinegary lady - husband more affable...looked like '49'er, generous with apples and information....on the road. High wind, ankle deep dust long monotonous road between miles of reaped yellow fields, parched and crying for rain - and fields of growing alfalfa. At four look for camp - nothing in sight except a single fringe of trees ½ mile to right, back of ranch house. Knocked at door, woman at first suspicious - then unbends, gives us milk and apples. Fringe of trees proves to be the bed of Arroyo Seco - Fine water in stone tower well in alfalfa fields - make camp in a clump of willows. Bed soft, alfalfa - night comes rapidly. big cheeful fire, sleep very well - coyotes and owls.

October 8

Margin notes:
- Coffee .15
- Onions .05
- 4.61

Break camp at dawn; marvelous cloud effects. Mists in hills, clear horizon clouds overhead, sprinkle of rain. Cross alfalfa fields to road. Reach Greenfield at 8 a.m. Buy coffee and onions. Leave road about 10 a.m. and reach river bed. Breakfast back of disused pig sty. Small piglets interested spectators M. develops new blister on old blister.
Cross river bed - dry - desert-like - heat shimmers -small whirlwind to the right. Rest on opposite side under large live oak six miles from King City. Make King city at 4 p.m. dusty and footsore - make a few purchases and seek camp near river. Difficulty about water - very dark - eat supper by campfire -hear tremendous howling of coyotes.   King City quite a burg;one main street,

Ruins of Soledad Mission

Desert stretch in Monterey County
Bed of Salinas River

Mary on Header-bed Wagon
Salinas Valley

October 9

[margin notes:
Hamburger .10
Pumpernickel .10
Beer (for the man) .10
Karo .15
Tomatoes —
Salt —]

Break camp late owing to M's sore feet. Saw horned toad. At trough front of saloon - several men - migrating workers, two of them blanket stiffs. One, oldest man "I've heard you many times near Howard st. Frisco" Lift on way to San Lucas in harrow bed wagon - wine - take picture. Resume road, very hot, dry, dusty. Make San Lucas 4 p.m. a forlorn dry town reminiscent of days of roaring cattle town -(picture) Ask direction of young man sitting on stone platform "I'm a stranger myself. Are you still speaking for the SLP (Socialist Labor Party)? Buy karo syrup and make toward river. River dry water at ranch Salt - tomato field contributes to supper. Bed somewhat hard.

October 10

[margin notes:
Tomatoes —
Watermelon .10
5 mutton Chops —
Can of fruit —
5.16]

Break camp early. Eat tomatoes and watermelon. Resume road Walk partly on road and partly on railroad tracks - cloudy morning M's foot very bad, a disappointment - deserted house, dry well, resume stony rail tracks. In ten minutes reach water tank side of road - Hobo jungle - two blanket stiffs, one under shade of tank their fire still smoldering. Blanket stiffs depart; we commence our lunch Hobo goes. After lunch wagon hobo arrives; a short, fat, greasy individual in tight trousers, round felt hat - two good horses, small black dog. Sets out his camp stove. Comes along one-armed hobo whom wagon hobo picked up - great flock of sheep, burro in the lead. Crawls under barbed wire - sheep follow - Two horrid buckboards, small dark driver come for water. M. asks a lift on account of foot. Leave for San Ardo. Sheep man proves to be Frenchman of far above average intelligence. Talk of art and literature and politics. Road of alkali dust, soon covered head to foot, hills both sides valley crowd closer. Lift all way to Brodley - mutton chops - fruit; stop near Brodley, cross river, lost ½ hour hunting good spot for tent. Fire for cooking -windstorm, sparks threaten conflagration - trouble controlling. Make fire down bank on sand - storm increases. M. down on sand struggling with supper R. up above fighting with tent. darkness and wind come quickly and ever more stormy..succeed with soup and coffee - give up frying chops. R. and I eat, eyes closed, sands stormier - increases. Take tent down and gulp coffee thrust things in knapsack and struggle up bank. Creep under tent which is somewhat protected by huge fallen poplar. Wind roars and dashes against tent, threatening demolition. Finally sleep. Waken, strange snarling sound very close - seems to be in opposite side of log at feet. Grasp knotted clubs and wait, snarls continue - puzzled - sounds like cat, but different. Last match, make little straw fire (wind storm had subsided, calm starlight. Snarls continue followed this time by hoo -hoo In branch overhead a large and indignant owl. Sleep well.

October 11

Morning calm and beautiful. grand breakfast, chops mush, fruit, coffee, pumpernickel. Leave owl camp at 11 a.m.

San Lucas – old California cattle town

Hobo Jungle at Water Tank – San Lucas

"Our Kitchen" in the Salinas River

Sugar .10
Bread —
From train cook
Dinner .60
Paso Robles .60
Tip to Otto .05

Meet brown-coated man who had asked us were we still talking for the SLP two miles beyond Brodley. Walk mile - his name Roe, was on committee; unemployed Frisco last winter - looking for job. Left us near bridge being repaird. Stop for drink at greek work train - get two slabs bread -- Men work ten hours @ 1.75 a day, no Sunday work. Company board $14. a month Stay under a tree take off shoes, eat lunch - bread, onion, and water. Very good Resume road to San Miguel. Auto passes, "want a lift" Sore feet tempt us. Take left to Paso Robles In passing see San Miguel Mission - good preservation - San Miguel bears all characteristics of old Spanish town, adobe, piazzas on houses, red tile roofs. Bare hills give place to tree clad. See walnuts and watermelons. See small train, consisting of two prairie schooners, old buggy, cattle and horses, also a dog. Water buckets on axles. First schooner, lanky diner lolling on seat, inside a comely young woman with red cheeked baby - and old buggy, an ancient, ruddy faced man - black goggles - riderless, saddled hose brings up rear. Walk into Paso Robles at 4:30 p,m. Band concert making hideous discords in park. Library on center of plaza. Hotel flanking upper end. Mediocre stores, expect drug stores which look prosperous. Dinner. Sign, Home Cooking does not repel us. Enter little garden; alley, dining room, canvas roof, effort made to give garden sppearance. Dinner surprisingly good and cheap. Gray haired cobbler in suspenders, takes order, calling same in loud imitation of hasher to kitchen. Soon sent away by irate frau, a plump, practical German woman. Otto takes father's place, Otto about 2½ feet high - carries a tray as wide as his length with skill of experienced hasher. Father solaces himself with phonograph, accompany sentimental songs. Hear domestic conversation through thin partitions, whole family receives payment. Camp within earshot of city under oak.

October 12 (Monday)

Breakfast .80
Candy .05
Supper .50
Soda .20

Breakfast at German's good but surprisingly dear. Stroll about town. Take hot sulfur bath, feel fine. Municipal baths leased to a couple who we find are socialists (real SLP) variety. Rent of baths so high they can't make wages. No outside assistance in conducting baths.

7.46 October 13

Apples —

Get up at sunrise, resume road south. Make Templeton, camp near road - make breakfast. Resume road - heat insupportable - stop in half hour under great hickory trees. House burnt down, abandoned orchard - get apples - Lift through Atascadero Colony (a land scheme)- Lewis, a magazine man publishes The Woman's World gives a share of oil stock with each yearly subscription. Bought this 20,000 acre tract at $35.00 per acre, sells at from $300 - 500 an acre, city and farms, foundation of administration building. Dept store laid, after leaving wagon resume hot dusty road - come to state highway camp at 3 p.m. decide to go no further.

Taking a lift in a conveyance of doubtful safety over the Cuesta Pass

From Santa Margarita to San Luis Obispo

View — Cuesta Pass

Old Chapel San Luis Obispo Mission

Wednesday October 14.

Salt Pork .10
Buckwheat flour .25
Cr. of Wheat .20

Resume road at 6 a.m. reach Santa Margarita at 8:30 a.m. make few purchases. Catch lift to San Luis Obispo through Cuesta Pass. Machine, an ancient "one horse shay" affair being put to a trial; a trip over dangerous grades. Thrilling view from summit, sublime. Mary becomes ill. Ask Spanish farmer to camp during heat of day - under his trees — repulsed, "Them's my trees!" Down the road a few yards, called back. Woman wants to know what is wrong. Mary calls them down. Get back to main road, drop exhausted by heat under fringe of cedars by side of road. Make breakfast - tea with whiskey for Mary. House on opposite side of road - extraordinarily hospitable Danes, Matheson by name. Call us in, Mr. M. hitches up takes us into town Ice Cream. Visit San Luis Mission.

Mission of Saint Louis the Bishop - 1772 - see hand embroidered (by Queen's court) clothes, gold braid, coats, hand beaten silver chalices, etc., Sheep's blood used in making cement. Russian samovar among relics, old cross. The guide a dirty, greasy youth wearing discarded shirt of a priest. hand tied in a dirty rag, interrupting his monotonous flow of information to snivel and draw back mucous into nose, idiotically devout, and talks by rote. Supper at Mathesons, who we find to be socialists of a peculiar kind, sleep in large tent in orchard.

October 15

Syrup —
1 egg donated —

Breakfast at Mathesons. Get syrup, on road at 8 a.m. Reach San Luis Obispo hot sulfur springs at 11 a.m. Find fine stove under tree - table and bench - good water. Make breakfast. Then in sight of fashionable hotel (our back up) Difficulty drying clothes.

October 16

dz. apples —
2 doz. potatoes —
Bread .10
Karo .15
Milk .10
Sugar .10
Clams —
Coffee Cake .10
Coffee .15
Salad oil .15

On road at 6:30 Apples and potatoes. Reach Pismo Beach. Large popular -now deserted) resort - pitch camp in tent city. Make purchases - breakfast - get clams, bucketful in 10 minutes -famous Pismo variety. Two pots full of real clam chowder. Eat to satiation! Perfect beach - hard level floor. Ex-bartender, of about 50 years, very sociable, locquacious - two years ago married Methodist girl in Los Angeles - happy until sister-in-law tries by drugs in coffee to cure him of smoking habit; became ill..divorced. Kid Smith - apparently Mexican - lives here in shack with 13 yr old son, a pretty Indian type. Kid Smith himself good looking, swarthy type seems about 26 , must be older. Gives us salt, pepper and cup. Sit around fire after dark, eat baked apples and baked clams. Phosphorous on sea. Kid Smith tells about himself Old maid at Wave Hotel to right, shame. Sleep badly on hard wood floor of tent frame.

Saturday October 17

Clams —
Cheese .10
Buns .08

Wake 7 a.m. Breakfast -m,m,m. Clouds rain. Move to new hotel under deserted pavilion. Put up nails, hang up clothes, blankets, pots, make fire, everything lovely and comfortable. Receive callers, our friend the ex-barkeeper. Tell him we are walking -notes we have bare feet "But you have shoes, don't you?" We assure him we have.

9.04

At parting informs us he has bread for sale. Two migratory men seek shelter of pavilion - talk with them. Had been in labor organizations - now plainly individualistic Recent changes in methods of threshing beans used to use goats, etc. Many men displaced by modern threshers. Often big threshers displaced by small gasoline ones operated by farmers and family. Go clamming and bathing - light rain falls.

October 18

Candy .05
Bread .10
Bacon .20

Break camp - note tide was within three feet of tent. Walk barefoot along beach, often to our knees in water to Oceana an abandoned wind swept resort. Wind makes breakfast difficult - Meet Kid Smith again - while eating breakfast he again appears asks "Have you lost anything?", produces my bag, containing entire finances of trip. Oceana would have been the end of our journey but for Kid Smith. Meet elderly migratory loaded down for one month's stay. Tells us of impositions on men working under contractors on state highway - Tricks in boarding - unlawful hours, withholding of pay, excessive board, etc. At town of Oceana buy bread of socialist baker - Mohr - never allows an out-of-worker to go away empty handed. known to all the hoboes on the coast. Camp that night deep among the willows on Arroyo Grande River.

October 19

Onions —
milk .10
Round steak .10
Hotcake flour .15
Karo .15
6 sausages —
spuds —

Take railroad tracks to Guadelupe. At Callerdid, a siding, get water from work train. Eat piece of bread and water. Stop under water tank at 10 a.m. at Bromley, make breakfast and are the marks of deep interest to the school "marm" and pupils of an adjacent country school house. All come out to see. It appears almost as though a special recess had been given in honor of the occasion -- a man and a woman cooking a meal near the roadside. Resume wagon road to Guadelupe - Large onion field - take on a supply of onions. Resume road. Discover we have taken wrong road - our informant gives us lift to Guadelupe. Learned that sons of Spanish one time owned all these broad acres, now working in fields for wages. Cross Santa Maria River to Guadelupe - in Santa Barbara county. Guadelupe is half Japanese population - Japs take contracts topping sugar beets at 1.25 per ton and digging and topping beets; work like lightning told often take fingers off. Japs also lease onion fields at $50 per acre, onions this year low price - 40¢ per sack. Bad year for growers. Make purchases in Guadelupe Italian butcher very talkative and sociable - shows us his plant, makes present if ½ dozen sausages. We buy ten cents round steak. Camp outside of town under cypress - heavy fog almost like rain, warm and snug in our tent. Grass bed, spuds.

October 20.

Breakfast .80
Tip .10
large squash —
6 apples —
Figs
1 candy
juicy watermelon —

10.79

On the road to Santa Maria - lift of three miles in automobile, bean thresher - Eat breakfast in restaurant so as to be ready to go back in machine for bean threshing. But no sunshine, therefore no threshing. Look about town - a neat, well built little place. Note: Heney to speak at Main and Broadway at 2 p.m. but we do not wait. Attempt to buy bread but 10¢ asked for a small sickly looking rye loaf.

Camp at San Luis Obispo Hot Sulfur Springs

Pismo Beach

Counting railroad ties

Union Palmer Oil Company
near Sisquoc Calif.

Oil Well
Union Palmer Oil Co.
near Sisquoc

Sugar .10
Bread .10

Postcards three and two for 5¢. Living seems high. Get information about oil wells at Palmer, take road towards Sisquoc - see old race course and paddocks. Get apples and squash - latter very large and heavy. foraging good; more apples, see figs R. jumps fence - while busy with figs an elderly lady comes out and calls us in to get apples and melon. Melon delicious. Squat on ground and easily do away with a large one. Lady's name Mrs. McKennon very kind and talkative....her 61st birthday. Take road, get lift in gravel wagon with man, half Indian and half Spanish - blue handkerchief on head under canvas hat, falling over shoulders. Man sad and heavy eyed, never been out of county feels the meagerness of his life. Meet another wagon driven by bearded, swarthy fellow - hails our driver in Spanish. turns to us both, talks in English - jocular - glib - goes on. He's ver' smart kid" wishful and admiring from our driver. Learn he was in Phillipines 6 years , came back unexpedectly to home with Filipina wife. Reach Gary, a forlorn cluster of houses among bare hills. Gary's store camp near school, get hay for bed - cold night warm in tent.

October 21

Pears
mush
6 spuds
Bread
Milk
Beans
Apples

Take road to Sisquoc - Pears - Reach large warehouse supplying oil fields. Buy mush, walk up toward Palmer Union Oil Fields. Stop to make breakfast back of ranch house. Discovered mush wormy; given mush by woman in house. Breakfast sumptiously - children - pictures. Leave things at house and walk to the oil fields - see drilling - take picture. On way back get a short lift. Young boy - informs us of conditions - English and German capital in oil. Boy works on county road - $ 1.25 a day and food, worked over 8 hours. Favors 8 hour law - thinks it will reduce unemployment. Take road toward Foxen Canyon - spuds- Camp that night in barn and make supper on stove - kindness of Mrs. Louis Holt - daughter of Billy Hobson -pioneer. Crossed plains in 1862, one of five children. Get milk and bread - apples and much kind information about roads. Mrs. Holt a camper herself and very sympathetic - husband an ex-oil driller now milks cows under wife's tutelage. She unconsciously feministic and paints china, as well as makes butter, milks cows, drives machine etc. Beans

October 22

Bread
Grapes

Leave Holts at 7 a.m. Stop to make breakfast in Foxen Canyon by stream. Wash hair, take picture - rest - resume road at 2 p.m. along winding canyon, here narrow and shallow; there deep and wide. Sky intensely blue, hills yellow, flicked with clumps of dark oak. (Grapes and melon before making breakfast camp, melon not ripe) At 3 p.m. come to Foxen - take pictures of horses threshing beans. Drill on towards Zaca ranch - steep grade to summit. Then on and on and finally at dusk come to Zaca Ranch House. No gates evident. Climb fence, air of inhospitality. Old lady at first house, indifferent reception - directs us to second house; return to first place. Plenty of short straw, prospects for good bed - make fire, old lady comes out and informs us not to sleep near straw on ground - fleas. In quandry, Arrival of nice stagey young gentleman dressed like cowboy, accompanied by three little girls.

Rudolph doing dishes and resting weary feet

Threshing beans with horses
Foxen Canyon

Santa Inez Mission

Road between Gaviota
and Santa Barbara

Santa Barbara

Does not like our fire. Mary talks to him - he retires vanquished
and baffled - get some bread from old lady, eat supper in dark,
lighted by very small fire. Crescent moon. Decide to pack up
after supper and walk to Los Olives. Take road winding palely
in dim moon and starlight at 7 p.m. Beautiful walk - arrive at
Los Olives at 9 p.m. "Widow's place." Stores closed, no candles,
seek hay stack in dark Find one - dogs bark. Sleep in great
haystack. Wonderful starlight.

Friday October 23

Mush	.20
Candles	.05
Bread	.10
Cookies	—
dr. apples	—
4 tomatoes	—
small cabbage	—
Salmon	.15
Karo	.15

Get up at sunrise. Very cold. Walk about Los O. pretty
little town nestled among the hills - picturesque little tavern.
Sit around waiting for grocery store to open. At 7 a.m. grocer
comes leisurely on scene. The widow comes in, morning cop, etc.
Some admirers present - gun incident. We buy mush and candles -
go up near schoolhouse - cook breakfast - observe children arriving,
teacher(man) comes in automobile, had lifted some children to
school - teacher plays marbles with children. Learn he has
taught here 14 years - has seven grades this year - 35 children.
At 9 a.m. resume road south - lift in mail car - stop at Santa
Inez Mission take pictures (pictures forbidden) visit the
Solvang colony - neat well built houses and store - branch library,
buy bread. Go on in machine to GaviotaPass. Leave machine, go
through pass, very steep grades. Apples, tomatoes, small cabbage.
Reach Los Cruces, a one time Spanish settlement, now broken down,
neglected, and enterprising Inn conducted by one Nichols. 100
yards further on make purchases at forlorn store kept in tiny, dark
room at Los Cruces, then go on about ½ mile - nothing to soften
bed this night. Rudolph in middle of night takes off his underwear,
strange itch - night warm, tender moon.

October 24

Hot Cake Flour	.15
Milk	.05
Soap	.10
Chocolate	.05
Soap (Rudolph)	.10
Santa Barbara	
Supper	1.25
Room	1.00

On road at 6:30 a.m. Pass through wonderful rocky gorge -
Reach Gaviota, an insignificant group of houses in the blazing sun,
by the sea at 8:30. See many migratories around station Buy
hot cake flour and milk - go across field towards spring down in
hollow. Find a perfectly equipped jungle - tables, rude chairs,
stove, straw, etc., We boil up , eat breakfast. Mend broken strap
on knapsack - make other repairs - read while clothes dry. Break
camp about 3 p.m. (Rudolph pays 10¢ for bar of soap).
    Same day - Dr. Saunders, veterinary - lift into Santa Barbara,
arrive at 8:30 dazzled by multiplicity of bright lights in street
and stores. Had passed by great walnut groves. Take supper in
restaurant. Walk about - leave films for developing. Hotel
The Anapamu - "Is this gentleman your husband?" Sleep at Hotel
Ruby $1.00.

Sunday October 25

Eggs	.30
2 sodas	.20
Postal Cards	.15
Stamps	.15
Supper	.80
	15.94

Out at 8 a.m. stroll about, buy eggs, go down by beach to make
breakfast - inconvenient place, close to boulevaRD _ Jones appears,
Go over to Shine Acres after breakfast, get permission to tent on
shore access. The Barkers nice, The Jones very nice, hospitable.
Visit Mission, light night good for pictures - sodas - supper .80¢
Waiter confused.

Mary
Santa Barbara Mission

Santa Barbara Mission
Father Michael

Arcades — Santa Barbara Mission

-11-

[Left margin notes:]
Lunch 26th
donated by
Lady Baptists
(Ice Cream
& cake)
milk .10
Sodas .20
Knorr .10
sugar .15
Chocolate .28
cheese .15
Bread .10
soda .20
salt
Bait .10
Root beer ——
6 Tomatoes ——
Lima Beans ——
1 sweet potato ——
nuts ——
2 dz. oranges ——
Hamburger
& Bacon .10
————
Candy .10

Supper .70

18.22

Monday October 26

    Breakfast very substantial - at Jones. Visit Mission take pictures Brother Michael - 50 ¢ expense. Visit Fly A American Film Co. studio and Portland genius. See picture produced "As a man thinketh" (Take pictures)- make purchases. Tea at Jones-contribute our bread and cheese.

October 27

    Breakfast at Jones - go fishing with Jones, not much luck, 5 or 6 fish. Disappointed about mail. Dinner at Jones. Chicken soup, fish, etc. Jones a machinist - wife, a large good looking blond woman - Jones tells us tales of the road, childhood, Molly Maguires, etc. (Take pictures) Resume road at 3 p.m. Road south with beautiful residences - see oil wells in sea in Sumerland. Reach Carpenteria. The Jersey man treats with beer, donates bottle root beer. Buy meat, seek camp. Find place in great olive grove - walnuts, oranges. Table chairs, enjoy luxurious meal from soup to nuts. Sleep on lima beans.

October 28

    Take road through Cassitas Pass. Lift over grades. Talk with IWW ranch hand, fears to carry card, Whitey OBreans Camp at Foster Park. Reach Ventura, an ugly uninteresting place - walk up railroad track, find camping place under eucalyptus trees on edge of lemon orchard. Sleep on straw. Trains during night

October 29

    Wake early, make breakfast. See town - mission not interesting. On road to Oxnard get lift on machine. Oxnard - American Sugar Co. town - large hotel - plaza - many stores, saloons, pool rooms, Japanese quarter - Mexican quarter communicates by gate with Sugar Co"s grounds. Office of Company refuse us. Rain comes. take short lift toward Camarillo. Learn factory about to close down season from July-August to Nov. 12 Hour shifts, 17¢ hour labor. Company owns only 1500 acres out of 22,000 acres but leases land buys up ranches steadily when possible. Stop for shelter at ranch owned by Company - poor reception -push on to Camarillo get there about 4 p.m. Beautiful church on hill - Mission style built by Camarillos - rich ranchers surrounding. Eat supper in Camarillo Restaurant - food surprisingly good and plentiful for money 35¢. Many diners - state highway crew, surveying gang, ranch hands, etc. Go out, dark rain descends again. Make for barn along r.r tracks. Skirmish about and slip in - dry and warm, bean straw, horses munching. Prepare to make ourselves comfortable - hear noises, 3 migratories seek barn-too dark to see their faces. We make ourselves known. Men very respectful. We sleep at one end they at other end, very well.

Studio
American Film Co.
Santa Barbara

Studio Scene
American Film Co
Flying "A"

Mary

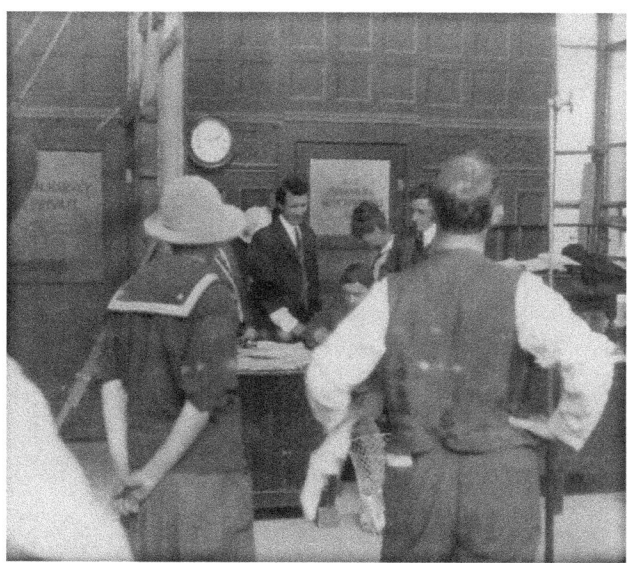

Mary watching

October 30

Cheese .10
Cakes .05
Suet .10
4 Tomatoes —

Wake at dawn, on road at 6 a.m. Roads muddy, thirsty and hungry. No water - Melon patch - melons look good, plug half a dozen, all unripe. Bitterly disappointed. Plod on towards Conejo Pass - see water tank and round concrete trough in field. R. climbs up tank - water no good - in troughs very dirty. Mary washes feet. We go on, still hungry and more thirsty than ever. Plod on for about a mile more. Machine passes - pauses further on - waits - and asks us if we wish to ride. We do. Pass, boldly beautiful, curves dangerous, hills bare, precepitous . Rach Calabases at 9.a.m. Leave machine. buy cheese. Lady in store tells us her woes. Buried mother and husband 6 weeks ago - very proud of funerals. We make breakfast under oak. Resume road 2 p.m. Lift on truck to Burbank, beautiful hills, fertile valleys. Buy cakes and salt pork. Camp on place near city. Lutge's place - an unkempt shiftless fat individual - idiot boy annoys - water witch. Burbank the horse breeder - damp, foggy night. alfalfa.

Saturday October 31

1 casaba —

Rise somewhat later than usual - wet - breakfast - on road towards Tropics. good road - casaba melon - Glendale, Lift in bumpety truck into outskirts of Los Angeles. Get off at Westlake Park - Keystone performers - park scene -- Mable Norman -- Roscoe Arbuckle - (take picture) -- arrive at headquarters 1 p.m. Meet comrades. Lenay takes us to home - eat there - gets room for us in neighborhood - hold street meeting - successful. Buy Rudolph new pants and shirt.

Sunday November 1st

After meeting
Supper .60

Rise at 9 a.m. go to headquarters stroll about. Hold hall meeting in evening Mary gives bum talk. We like Roadhouse - Leroy, etc., (Sunday night we buy a steak).

Monday November 2

Postcards
& Stamps .20
Movies .20
Beach
expenses 1.75
2 Films .35
Development .60

Mary washed clothes. R. goes with Leroy and Phister to Eagle Rich Park. M. goes with the females to Eastlake Park. The Fisher's come after supper. At 8:30 R and I escape - take a walk, see Odyssey of The North - sleep well.

November 3

We go with Mrs. Leroy and kid to Venice. Pleasure some-what spoiled kid but make the best of it. Stay downtown in evening. Election night We see Remond, seems to be nearly gone, tuberculosis. R and I go with the Roadhouses to theatre after which supper at Tuan Hall Cafe. Get to bed late.

November 4

Steak .60

Rise late - Breakfast - Headquarters - spend day at Roadhouses. See factory - M. goes with ladies to Animal Farm; weather excessively hot. Meeting downtown in evening. Slip away after meeting to be alone. Eat

Studio Scene
American Film Co.
Santa Barbara

Keystone Film Company
Los Angeles

Mable Norman   Roscoe "Fatty" Arbuckle

Mable Norman Roscoe "Fatty" Arbuckle

-13-

movie .10
Refreshments .30

Thursday November 5

    Visit library - movie - late for dinner. Go to San Pedro hold good meeting.

Friday November 6th

Lunch .35
Movies .20
Carfare .20
Papers .10
Late supper .80

    Go to Exposition Park. Leroy brings Schoen home to supper. Talk over old times. Go to Section . Eat late lunch. Take walk in evening.

November 7

Lunch .65

Lunch at noon. Angel's Flight - Library. Meeting evening, very successful - Dance at Headquarters. Take late walk with Schoen. Tamales (canned)

Sunday November 8

Room 1.00

Dinner at Weiss's. Redmond collected $22.+odd. *change.* R. very happy. Starts for San Bernadino tomorrow. Anaheim comrades - Janson, Miles, invite us. bad incident - no room for his wife. I take walk with Mrs. Janson - Leave at 7:30 Mrs. J. rides. Politely refuse comrade Janson's hospitality. Rent room Palace Hotel $1.00 Rains heavy during night.

Monday November 9   (sick)

Walnuts —
Berries —
Oranges —
Room .75

    Go over to Jansens = breakfast coffee and ---Miles entertains on violin. Walk out to pepper fields - half promise at Mauerhen - forage walnuts and oranges - few blackberries. Weather continues threatening - walk back to Jansens; he is a vulgar boozer, his wife a poor thin, half crazy creature in fear of everbody, including a strapping blond female who runs the store. Mrs. J. with fearful mein makes us coffee - such a shiftless cruel bunch. Decline invitation to supper made by Mrs. J. who apparently has no rights here. Walk about town for about two hours. Sit on steps of library waiting for evening opening. Read til nine then go to room at Palace Rooming House. Rains furiously all night.

Tuesday November 10

Breakfast .65
Potatoes .10
Onions .05
Mush .10
garlic .05
Karo .15
milk .10
Macaroni .10
Salami .50
Peanut butter .05
Coffee .15
Knorr Soap .20
apron .59
Hair Pins .05
Mirror .05

    Breakfast at restaurant - make purchases - weather doubtful. Feel a little despondent. Take road to pepper ranch of Mauerhan. Get there at noon. Prepare to make camp in damp ground in Walnut orchard. Get tent up when Mauerhan tells us we can use shack on premises - old carpenter politely but firmly ousted. Shack new and clean. We make ourselves at home then go to town to make a few purchases Go back in Mauerhan's machine. Eat cheerful supper, clean up and go to bed. Clear night.

Rudolph

Chili Pepper Strings   Anaheim

Mary

Wednesday 11 November

Margin notes: Bread —, ½ dozen donuts —

Morning cloudy - finish breakfast at 7 a.m. Put to work. I sort peppers all day. R. Told he is to get 20¢ per hour. I worked 8 hours, R. 9 hours. After supper clean up thoroughly cob webs and all. Write cards - take after dinner walk. Take sponge bath. Tired. Go to bed at 9 p.m.

November 12

Rise at 6 - R. commences work at 7 - Mary 7:30. R. does various things - Mary sorts. Weather clears - knock off at noon one hour - cook macaroni and chocolate. Mrs. Mauerhan brings stuffed peppers and puddings. (Take pictures.) I work with Mrs. Kaley, a thin, pale, little down-easterner. from Freeport Illinois. Bought ten acres here, oranges and peppers - live in their garage, have not built yet-- both work for wages, as well as farm their land whenever possible.

November 13

Margin notes: 2 bread —, Pie —

M. sorted on strings all day. Get 15¢ per hour but allowed milk, etc., gratis. Foggy and chilly. Eat hearty supper, retire early. Shift bed to floor.

Saturday November 14

Margin notes: Tomatoes 14th, Peppers —, Anaheims, Ham .85, Beef .15, Potatoes .10

Mary sorts trays, very tired, but try to make 9 hours - work gives out at 4 p.m. Rudolph makes 9 hours. M. gets supper early - everything cooked spanish - tomatoes and chillies being plentiful. Get paid M. $5.03 R. 7.20 = $12.73 four days. After supper go to town buy groceries. visit Jansens bakery. Go to bed late. M. had finished work with a severe headache - walked it off.

Sunday November 15

Margin notes: Cr. of wheat .20, Chocolate .30, Coffee .30, Sugar .25, Soap .05, Macaroni .15, 1 bread —, 1 pie —, ½ dz cookies —, large rye —, Coffee cake —

Rise at 7:30 Breakfast at 8:30. Wash clothes and clean house. Get table, arrange things - cook spanish beef stew and boil ham- folks gone pick large mess of raspberries - take bath dine sumptiously Take walk, forage large bag of walnuts, one oranges, beans. Beautiful day, starlight night lucky walk home, forage beans. Dark when we get home - cook pot of chocolate - lunch on cold baked ham, tomatoes, and chocolate. Bed at 9:30 p.m.

Monday November 16

Margin notes: Candy —, 15¢, Raspberries —, Tomatoes —, Milk —

Fresh morning milk - M. strings today. Hard work at 5¢ a string. Made 16 strings, fingers sore. Retire at 7 p.m. Fine supper tonight, macaroni, boiled ham tomatoes, chillies, nuts and chocolate.

Tuesday November 17

Margin notes: 1 orange —, beans —, newspaper .05, sodas .20

Mary strings all morning - eleven strings - fingers very sore - Mexicans laugh and talk much at their work. M. sorts strings in

River Bottom at San Juan Capistrano

On the road mile above San Juan Capistrano

(margin notes:)
1/2 lb bread
1 small [bread]
1/2 doz donuts
1 coffee cake

afternoon - has an idea Mrs. M. and Ida have a dislike for her. All begins to jar on us very much. narrow people, all of them. Rudolph works in chilli mill all afternoon _ Chilli dust very annoying. After supper take warm sponge. Retire at 9:30.

November 18

M. strings all morning. R. works time all morning. Strings in afternoon - 33 strings together, all told. Santa Ana wind prevents emptying houses. It seems that Mrs. M. is looking for an excuse to get rid of us. We take care to give her none. Mrs. Wylie appears.

November 19

(margin:)
Bread —
Coffee cake —

Talk and laughter of the Mexicans at the strings hushed. Annoyed at the fast pace of the Americanos. We all string - R. and I make 64 strings. Mrs. W. makes 38 alone. Santa Ana wind continues.

(margin:)
6 donuts
Tomatoes
Milk   .20
Milk —
Nuts —
Can milk .10
soup   .20
mush   .20
shave   .15
Shoe
strings .05
Films   .35
21st
Oil Shoes .10
Oranges —
Round
steak   .15

Saturday November 21

Beyond Tustin, enroute to San Juan Capistrano

Resting under great eucalyptus at edge of orange grove, eating orange and writing. Have just finished breakfast and packed up - now resting . Yesterday (Friday) Mauerham informed us he just close down on chillies because of countermanded orders. We feel he is lying but now in the possession of almost $23. we feel ready for anything again. Went to Anaheim, made purchases visited the bakery. On the road at 3 p.m. Meet Billings on road (a neighbor of Mauerham) and hear intersting facts concerning Mauerham's business methods. Camp in creek bottom near Santa Ana. Saturday morning rise at dawn. Go through Tustin - make breakfast under eucalyptus just beyond oranges. Get auto lift with couple who tell of their experiences in desert. Lost for three days in autos - ride with them to El Toro. Walk on to San Juan Capistrano. Arrive at dusk..real Spanish town - adobe houses no gas or electricity. Butcher, candle, glasses, matches, buy 15¢ steak. Make hurried march down road to creek construction camp - go up creek, forced to ford it. Make camp near haystack. Visitors - knights of the road, one apparently a scandinavian - had been in Portland during fight. He knew him, we recognize him.

November 22

(margin:)
Milk .10
Karo .15
Bread .05
3 meals .75

Making fire when an invitation to breakfast is called from construction camp. Eat in cook shack. Break camp at 9 a.m. Very picturesque mission. Talk with two ladies about transporting art,etc. At restaurant eat chilli con carne. Meet boss of skinners from camp, treat him to meal. Take road late afternoon. Get lift to Oceanside - our host Alaska man   camp that night on beach Sleep fine.

Monday November 23

(margin:)
Films .35
Candy .05
Bread .05

Breakfast - bath - lunch - on road at 2:30 - long smooth road great blue expanse of sea, dry country. Walk until dark. Find house that is not deserted - camp - (Many abandoned houses along here) After

Mission San Juan Capistrano

supper visit the Davis's (where we got water) She is a very bright young woman. Lived in Colorado during Cripple Creek strike. Mr. Davis an oil driller - large heavy young man - dull - Hard round that night.

November 24

Apples .10
Garlic .05
Bread .05
Tomato Sauce .05
Chocolate .35
Milk .05
Bread .05
Chops .20

Take road at 7:30. At Encinatos buy apples and bread. No breakfast yet - accept lift to LJolla - truck breaks down - we help with suggestions. M.'s assistance valuable. After awhile resume road. Leave truck at fork in roads, resume coast road to LaJolla about five miles on - hot - hungry - tired. See LaJolla from height at end of rocky point, camp under cliff on beach. Fishers - have trouble about wood. Eat breakfast, rest, go on - View caves and cliffs at LaJolla - camp in empty field, hay that night.

November 25

25th
Coffee .15
Beans .15
Hot Cake Flour .15
Spaghetti .10
Sugar .15
Milk .15
Figs & Prunes .25
Bacon .25
Butter .46
Rolls .10
Tom. Sauce .05
Potatoes .10
Celery .05
Cheese .10
Herring .10
Bread .10
Meat .20
Cheese .15

Reach San Diego at 8:30 - meet Hertzbrun - go to Gusts Bookstore - meet comrades. Rent room at 839 Front St., $2.75 a week. Buy groceries - get letters from home and Jack. Grists have reference to my law aspirations.

Thursday November 26

Thanksgiving day - warm clear blue skies - eat Thanksgiving dinner of veal stew and celery - delightful - go out to see San Diego Mission, Mission Cliffs, see beaches - Lunch Warm evening - movies.

Saturday November 28

Went to Exposition Grounds - cloudy - (took only three pictures.) Walk about town in evening. Movies.

Sunday November 29

26th
Movies .20
Drinks .15
Beer .80
Bread .10
27th
Apple Butter .35
Rolls & Cake .15
Donuts .05
Stamps .15
28th
Prunes, Figs .25
Bread .10
Films .70
Bread .10
Fish .10
Movies .10
Ham .20

Go to Coronado Beach - clear day - (take two pictures.) Down to $7.40 and Frisco 600 miles away. Visit science class at SP HQ meet SLP comrade Fred Moore R. and I take a walk. Eat hamburger at "Charlie's Place".

Monday

Tuesday December 1

Learn about lemon picking. Hopes raised. Go out to Upas St to look up Dick. Rain, beautiful rainbow in canyons. Find Dick has gone to S.A, separated from wife. Visit Kirk's Law School in evening Nothing doing on lemon line. Meet Comrade Sachs. Are persuaded to stay a day or two longer.

29th
Carfare .20
Cookies .05

42.56

La Jolla

Oceanside

Entrance to
San Deigo Exposition

Exposition Building

One of the buildings at the
San Deigo Exposition

On the way to Mission Dam

Old Mission Dam San Deigo

Expenses 1.00 Wednesday December 2

    Break our last fiver.

December 3

    Meet a Mrs. Hilquowitch in Grists Bookstore - hear P. Kovitch has ranch in Mission valley. Decide to look him up. We organize section at Tuttle's home. 13 charter members.

Friday December 4

    Go out with Mr. Beihl Kovitch has 30 acres pretty little bungalow. Call at Beihl's after supper.

December December 5

    Tramp about - go up canyon to springs. Visit Hilquovitches - argument.

Sunday December 6

    Go with Beihl and his son, Joe, up Pass - see old Mission dam. Go back over rocks through river bed. Have dinner at Beihls. Go to Greists for supper. Drive in Meeting that night. Girl named Ruth Coward talks - we take floor. P. Kovitch displeased. We feel a little warm about it and decide to cut our visit short. On way back in car rain comes. However before we reach stables weather clears. Drive back in beautiful moonlight. Cold . Beihl persists like a "knvechen-kopf" to keep up the argument

Monday December 7

    Slight coolness between us and Kovitch - melts, however. Tea at Beihls in evening. Kovitch tells of inception of Zionist Movement. Romantic story of first Russian immigration to America.

Tuesday December 8

    Breakfast . Beihls come over. Hot argument. Leave at 9 a.m. Mary becomes sick. Beihl boys inflict themselves on us in long walk to canyon. Take car - transfer at Mission Cliffs. Get some Jamaican ginger. Get room at Mrs. Young's. See Grist. Meet Neilson Collier on street. M. rests all afternoon. Borrow $5.00 from Grist.

December 9

    Sleep late - go out for breakfast. Visit Tuttle. Spend day walking about visiting Grist and reading. Take the "Governor" at 11 p.m. for Los Angeles - very smooth trip.

On the hills
at Mission Valley
San Deigo

P. Kovitch's Ranch
Mission Valley San Deigo

Mission Valley San Deigo

Thursday December 10.

Arrive at San Pedro at 7 a.m. Rain - Breakfast on boat. Get into town at 9 a.m. Letter from Redmond - something in the air here, about Schoen - Roadhouse etc. Call up Roadhouse - go to Beardstown at noon. Roadhouse gives us both work. Will make our expenses back to San Francisco. Go to section meeting. Trouble easily smoothed for time being.

Friday December 11

Wake at 6:30 a.m. Report for duty at factory. M. brushes, R. general helper at furnaces. R 25¢ and hour M. 15¢ per hour. Mrs. Roadhouse feeds us wonderfully - We play cards in evening.

Saturday December 12

Work half day. Help clean house in afternoon. At 4 p.m. Rudolph and Roadhouse go down town for shave.

"To regret one's experiences is to regret one's own development."

Expenses Other than food.—

Date	Item	Amount
9/26	dozen films	.70
9/28	" "	.35
	Zinc ointment	.10
10/3	Fry Pan	.25
	Stockings	.50
	Coffee Pot	.25
	Tin cup	.05
	Development & Printing	.70
	Films	.70
10/9	½ yd Cheesecloth	.05
	blue handkerchief	.10
10/11	Films @ Paso Robles	.70
10/12	Stockings	.25
	Cards, stamps	.20
	oil cloth for camera	.15
	Tin Plate	.05
	Development & Prints	.85
10/14	Film - San Luis Obispo	.70
	Mission trip	.10
10/17	Hair Pins	.05
10/19	Zinc Ointment	.10
	Washcloth	—
	new skin	—
10/26	Mission trip Santa Barbara	.50
10/28	Film (Ventura)	.35
10/29	Postal Cards & Stamps	.10
10/31	Pants Rudolph	1.25
	Shirt	1.00
	Carfare	.10
		10.20

San Diego Mission

Coronado Hotel, Coronado

If ever you go on a long tramp, I would advise first of course, a pair
of stout boy's shoes, strong but not too heavy, and then wear first
a pair of woolen socks, natural color, over this strong ribbed boy's
stockings. Had I done this at the start, I would have saved myself
many painful days. I got the proper shoes, but wore only one pair of
stockings, thus leaving too much room in the heel. There is bound
to be a certain amount of friction anyway, but this is very much mini-
mized if the socks are worn under the stockings.

We woke at the first streaks of dawn. The morning was
cold, the sharp air fresh with the pungent and oders of pine and
redwood. Far off, could be heard the last Hoo-Hoo of a belated Owl,
and all about the stirrings of the birds of the sunlit hours.

We threw back the flaps of the tent and dressed. Our heels were raw
and to draw on our shoes was exceedingly painful. I tore into strips
two large white handkercheifs I had fortunately brought along,
and sprinkeling them with Talcum powder(which was all we had), we
bound them around our heels, drawing the stockings over this bandage.
(Wash in cold stream)
Rudolph quickly made a fire and in a few moments, we had
a big pot of mush boiling and bubbling. A fine breakfast was made of
mush, hot cakes, honey, bacon and coffee. By this time, the sun be
gan to send its golden shafts down through the lofty Redwoods. Looking about we could see that we had stumbled upon a little natural glade,
xxxxxxxxxxxxxxxxxxxxxxx, the grass was thick and of delicate blades,
the, the brown fronds of dead ferns reflected themselves in the stream
that, and all about was a silence, so solemnly sweet, that we unconscialy
hushed our voices when we spoke.

After breakfast, we xxxxxxxxxxxxxxxxx we washed our towel
and handerchiefs and while these were drying, we wasked the pots and
other things, and packed the knapsask, rolled the tent and I mended a
tear in my skirt and one in R's trousers.

We made a late start, (11 A.M.) because of the pain in our
heels, and then we took up the trail where we had left it the previous
evening. We walked through the great aisles between the giant Redwod
following the Creek, and came upon
the Inn at the place called Governor's Camp, which was by the way, in
no way official. The Inn, a conventional Log Cabin affair, was
situated in a great sunny glade, and was sourrounded by bungalows,
and tents, which at this time of year were almost deserted. This
pleased us immensely. We asked the direction to Boulder Creek,
and being averse to mingle with the human animal, preferring our
own company and solitude, we struck out immediately. But we had
not gone far, when the clear cool waters of the creek tempted us.
We were deep in the forest again, although a wide and well tramped
path ran along the creek with its danger of pedestrians. But it
was late in the season and we took a change. Selecting a particularly
secluded spot all overhanging with vines and ferns, we threw aside
our buddens, and xxxxxxxxx while R. watche , I stripped and bathed
in the tingling cold waters. (the day had grown very warm) and then
R. bathed while I bwatched. After bathing we dressed and ten rested
with our feet in the water for about an hour or so. But we had to be
on our way. We hoped to make Boulder Creek that night. There we cod
could get some ointment for our blisters.

For about a half hour, walking was painful, but after that we walked more easily. The bath had refreshed us very much. The trail led us through a deserted Mill Camps, . The ruined sheds, decaying and weather stained piles of lumber, deserted bunk houses, and empty stalls, there baked in the hot rays of the sun, in a short of a spell, and it seemed as though there were ghostly presences all about and as though the imprisoned buzz of the saws would be released at any moment.

We explored the place, arrived at satisfactory conclusions, as to why the place had been abandoned, and under what conditions it would pay to resume the operation of the place, and then we pushed on, up a steep rough road, and over a very rickety bridge, the supports rotten and the boards all lose, this crossing quite a respectable chasm.

At the top of this road, we came upon a large aple orchard, the first we has seen, and you can imagine the aples made our mouths water. R, was about to enter the orchard, but I fresh with my city moralites said no, let us ask. The old Irish farmer, granted us enthusiastic permission, pointing out the best trees. We ate our fill of the juciest mountain aples I hav e ever eaten, then I filled up my Linen bag, which I had made just for this purpose, foraging.

We could not refuse the old farmer's invitation to walk over to 'is house to see some 'wonderful' furniture that he had made from Redwood Burl, and then after a half mile walk we came to the Divide. Way down in the blue depths was Boulder Creek.

You will remember Berta, when you were at Boulder Creek, te mountains to your right coming to Boulder Creek. That 'i where we now were. Fortunately for us it was now an all down grade. But even in spite of that we did not make boulder creek that night. We were still two miles East of it, when darkness began to ascend. There was no water, the little water in the creed at this point was stagnant, and it looked as though we would hav to go supperless. We had not yet been taught by necessity that there are times when you must go to people's houses a d ask for water. We saw one vacant house, and climbed over t e fence, but found no water there. Another five minues around the bed of the road, revealed a big treught overr unnig with water, and a big sign, "NO CAMPING- KEEP OUT". Of course, this at once advertised that it was very desirable as a camping place, and we went behind the trees and with great sighs of releif pulled off our shoes. In a half hour, we had our camp pitched and supper almost ready. The apple Sauce of which we made a big pot full took the long est to cook. A d it was delicious. Before we went to bed , we had apples again, baked.

When we were about to lie down, I had a premonition. We lit a candel and looked. Sure enough we had put up the tent in a bed of poison oak. We shifted it and slept, the sleep of the hiker.

Tuesday, Sept. 28th.

Next morning we awoke at Sunrise. Under the Tan oaks it was still very~~dark~~ dusky, but in the skies were the soft dawn streaks. It was cool but by the time we had the fire made, the mush cooked and the coffee boiled, the sun was filling the little valley with its golden warmth.

Loath to draw on our shoes, we lingered over our breakfast, adding a course of Hot Cakes to the rest. By the time we had finished, given our heels a sterile dressing, packed the knapsack and rolled the blankets, it was ten o'clock.

We made the two miles to Boulder Creek very slowly. Arrived there, we found the place improved since we had seen it last two years before, by the addition of a fine new hotel. We found the drug store, bought a box of Zinc Ointment and film, then looked up the bakery, and found the same man who two years ago had served us with cold grey coffee, still behind the counter. Bought a loaf of bread and lipped our way to the little Fern Brook of fond memorey, a mile or so below.

We found it, the same laughing brook, down in the cool shadows, the same ferns and the same irate lady in blue gingham who appeared above on the top of the bank and warned us not to destroy her ferns. It was delightful, and the lady must have been somewhat taken aback by my involuntary reply, "Oh, yes, we know, you said the same thing to us two years ago".

We lunched royally on Bread, Salami, apples and cool, water from the Brook, then bathed our feet, dressed our heels in Zinc Ointment and assured each other that our ~~feet~~ they felt fine. On the road, again, we had to confess that this was not so. If we could only make Felton, there was a harbour for a two or three days rest for our feet. But Felton was seven long cruel miles away.

Wagons passed and when they did, we stopped and admired the scenery, so that our painful plight would not be observed. Such are the silly contradictions of human nature, that we feared to be offered what we desired most in the world at that time, a lift. And so we admired the scenery, waited for the wagon to passed and then toiled on.

One time we saw a light cart appraching. We looked at eachother sighed, and turned to look down into the bed of the San Lorenzo, two hundred feet below. The cart apprached and, stopped We turned and were greeted by the young man driving. He seemed to know us, addressed us by name. We were surprised, of course, but thought he was a Feltonite whom we could not place. But he proved instead to be one of the thousands who had heard us at our Street meetings in Frisco. We talked a few minutes, then he prepared to drive on. Of course, seeing that we were hiking, he naturally thought that we wanted to keep on walking. Almost before I knew it, I burst out, "Are you going as far as Felton?" "Yes, passing it though it to Uchels". "Well, we will ride with you,

The drive along the familiar Santa Cruz road was full of pleasure, and recalled the many pleasant incidents of two years before.

We drove into Felton at just four o"clock and their, climbing out of the machine at the grocery store(by the way young Russell has sold out and is in the automobile business in Santa Cruz)were Mrs. Silberly (Kelpie) and Mrs. Slikerman. They seemed very glad to see us and Mrs. Slikerman learning of our crippled condition insisted that we stay with her until we felt ready to go on. We rode up to the gate in the grocery wagon and that evening we ate supper in the glass room and that night we slept under the Madrones and Redwoods on a couch placed out there.

We spent two pleasant days up on the hill in the little house up on the hill again delighting our eyes with the view of the hills and forests, and the little village nestling in the misty valley below. We visited our friends of old. The Solunds Solunds were delighted to see us. They in the mean while allied with the Germans,(the Guentners) by the marriage of Mrs. Solunds Deanie and the eldest German girl, who at the time of our visit was about to become a mother.

We learned that after all that hard work, the farm German's little farm has not been a success and that the place at Echels has suffered two fires. The German boys, bright and energetic, some of them grown men and some of them almost grown, are becoming very discontented and restless under the hard unpaid work of all these years and the country life barren of all the pleasures that healthy imaginative natures crave. The old man is suffering all the time with Malaria and well, they do not line up in a row, directed by the father and ing as they did two years ago. We had two very lively evenings all together

Did I tell you that the Kelpie has found new victims and is now running the Toll House Tavern? Soft drinks only and help articles. Yes, and she looks very blooming.

Tuesday, Sept. 28th.

Next morning we awoke at sunrise. Under the Tan oaks it was still dusky, but in the skies were soft dawn streaks. It was cool but by the time we had the fire made, the mush cooked and the coffee boiled, the sun was filling the little valley with its golden warmth.

Loath to draw on our shoes, we lingered over our break fast, adding a course of Hot Cakes to the rest. By the time we had finished, given our heels a sterile dressing, packed the knapsack and rolled the blankets, it was ten o'clock.

We made the two miles to Boulder Creek very slowly. Arrived there, we found the place improved since we had seen it last two years before, by the addition of a fine new hotel. We found the drug store, bought a box of Zinc Ointment and film, then looked up the bakery, and found the same man who two years ago had served us with cold grey coffee, still behind the counter. Bought a loaf of bread and limped our way to the little Fern Brook of fond memorey, a mile or so below.

We found it, the same laughing brook, down in the cool shadows, the same ferns and the same irate lady in blue gingham who appeared above on top of the bank and warned us not to destroy her ferns. It was delightful, and the lady must have been somewhat taken aback by my involuntary reply, "Oh, yes, we know, you said the same thing to us two years ago."

We lunched royally on Bread, Salami, apples and cool, water from the Brook, then bathed our feet, dressed our heels in Zinc Ointment and assured each other that they felt fine.

On the road, again, we had to confess that this was not so. If we could only make it to Felton, there was a harbour for a two or three days rest for our feet. But Felton was seven long cruel miles away.

Wagons passed and when they did, we stopped and admired the scenery, so that our painful plight would not be observed. Such are the silly contradictions of human nature, that we feared to be offered what we desired most in the world at thatntime, a lift. And so we admired the scenery, waited for the wagon to passed and then toiled on.

One time we saw a light cart approaching. We looked at eachother and sighed, and turned to look down into the bed of the San Lorenzo, two hundred feet below. The cart approached and, stopped. We turned and were greeted by the young man driving. He seemed to know us, addressed us by name. we were surprised, of course, but thought he was a Feltonite whom we could not place. But he proved instead to be one of the thousands who had heard us at our street meetings in Frisco. We talked a few minutes, then he prepared to drive on. Of course, seeing that we were hiking, he naturally thought that we wanted to keep on walking. Almost before I knew it, I burst out, "Are you going as far as Felton?" "Yes, passing it through to Eckels".

The drive along the familiar Santa Cruz road was full of pleasure, and recalled the many pleasant incidents of two years before.

We drove into Felton at just four o"clock and their, climbing out of the machine at the grocery store (by the way young Russell has sold out and is in the automobile business in Santa Cruz) were Mrs. Silberly (Kelpie) and Mrs. Slikerman. They seemed very glad to seen us and Mrs. Slikerman learning of our crippled condition insisted that we stay with her until we felt ready to go on. We rode up to the gate in the grocery wagon and that evening we ate supper in the glass room and that night we slept under the Madrones and Redwoods on a couch placed out there.

We spent two pleasant days up in the little house up on the hill again delighting our eyes with the view of the hills and forests, and the little village nestling in the misty valley below. We visited our friends of old. The Solunds were delighted to seen us. They by the way are now allied with the Germans, (the Guentners) by the marriage of Mrs. Solunds Deanie and the eldest German girl, who at the time of our visit was about to become a mother.

We learned that after all that hard work, the German's little farm has not been a success and that the place at Echels has suffered two fires. The German boys, bright and energetic, some of them grown men and some of them almost grown, are becoming very discontented and restless under the hard unpaid work of all these years and the country life barren of all the pleasures that healthy imaginative natures would crave. The old man is suffering all the time with Malaria and well, they do not line up in a row, directed by the father and sing as they did two years ago. We had two lively evenings all together

Did I tell you that Kelpie has found new victims and is now running the Toll House Tavern? Soft drinks only and kelp articles. Yes, and she looks very blooming.

walked more easily. The bath had refreshed us very much. The trail led us through a deserted Mill Camp, . The ruined sheds, decaying ad weater stained piles of lumber, deserted bunk houses, and empty stalls, there under the hot rays of the sun, in a short of a spell, and it seemed as thought there were ghostly presences all about and as though the imprisoned buzz of the saws would be released at any moment.

We explored the place, arrived at satisfactory conclusions, as to why the place had been abandoned, and under what conditions it would pay to resume the operation of the place, andthen we pushed on, up a steep rough road, and over a very rickety bridge, the supports rotten and the boards all lose, this crossing quite a respectable chasm.

At the top of this road, we came upon a large apple orchard, the first we has seen, and you can imagine the apples made our mouths water. R, was about to enter the orchard, but I fresh with my city moralities said no, let us ask. The old Irish farmer, granted us enthusiastic permission, pointing out the best trees. We ate our fill of the juiciest mountain apples I have ever eaten, then I filled up my Linen bag, which I had made just for this purpose, foraging.

We could not refuse the old farmer's invitation to walk over to his house to see some wonderful furniture that he had made from Redwood Burl, and then after a half mile walk we came to the Divide. Way down in the blue depths was Boulder Creek.

You will remember Bertha, when you were at Boulder Creek, the mountains to your right coming to Boulder Creek. That is where we are now were. Fortunately for us it was all now down grade. But even in spite of that we did not make boulder creek that night. We were still two miles east of it, when darkness began to ascend. There was no water, the little water in the creek at this point was stagnant, and it looked as though we would have to go supperless. We had not yet been taught by necessity that there are times when you must go to other people's houses and ask for water. We saw one vacant house, and climber over the fence, but found no water there. Another five minutes around the bed of the road, revealed a big trought overrunning with water, and a big sign, "NO CAMPING- KEEP OUT". Of course, this at once advertised that it was very desirable as a camping place, and we went behind the trees and with great sighs of relief pulled off our shoes. In a half hour, we had our camp pitched and supper almost ready. The apple sauce of which we made a big pot full took the longest to cook. And it was delicious. Before we went to bed, we had apples again, baked.

When we were about to lie down, I had a premonition. We lit a candle and looked. Sure enough we had put up the tent in a bed of poison oak. We shifted it and slept, the sleep of the hiker.

OBITUARIES

Mary R. Schwab — Attorney Who Made S.F. History

Mary Rantz Schwab, the first female assistant city attorney in San Francisco, has died at her home in Walnut Creek at age 99.

Mrs. Schwab was sworn into office by Mayor James Rolph in an elaborate ceremony in 1923.

"I believe the world's work will be done better in the future because complete humanity, including man's energy, intelligence and psychology has combined with the same feminine forces to do the job," she said then. "Male energy alone has proved inadequate."

Mrs. Schwab was also an accomplished painter, and some of her friends affectionately called her the "Grandma Moses of San Francisco."

Born in Libinsk, Russia, she immigrated to the United States at age 5 and sold newspapers on the streets of Philadelphia at age 6. At 15 she left school to become a factory worker.

Mrs. Schwab arrived in San Francisco in 1911 and a year later married Rudolph Schwab, a social reformer and poet who died five years later.

She entered night classes at the San Francisco Law School in 1918, although she had no more than a grammar school education. She was graduated at the top of her class of four women and 72 men in 1922.

She served one year in the city attorney's office and later went into private practice.

During the Depression she organized an art class that became the nucleus for Bay Area artists involved in Works Progress Administration projects.

Mrs. Schwab, who died last Wednesday, is survived by two sisters, Berta Rantz of Walnut Creek and Celia Rantz Clark of San Francisco, and two brothers, Jock Rantz of San Francisco and retired Colonel Richard C. Rantz of Bellingham, Wash.

At her request, no funeral was held.

ABOOKS

ALIVE Book Publishing and ALIVE Publishing Group
are imprints of Advanced Publishing LLC,
3200 A Danville Blvd., Suite 204, Alamo, California 94507

Telephone: 925.837.7303
alivebookpublishing.com

www.ingramcontent.com/pod-product-compliance
Lightning Source LLC
Chambersburg PA
CBHW061419090426
42743CB00026B/3495